YOUR WORD IS FIRE

YOUR WORD IS FIRE

The Hasidic Masters
on Contemplative Prayer

Edited and Translated with a New Introduction by

Arthur Green & Barry W. Holtz

A JEWISH LIGHTS
Classic Reprint

JEWISH LIGHTS Publishing
Woodstock, Vermont

Your Word Is Fire: The Hasidic Masters On Contemplative Prayer
Copyright © 1993 by Arthur Green and Barry W. Holtz

Library of Congress Cataloging-in-Publication Data
Your word is fire: the Hasidic masters on contemplative prayer/ edited and translated by
Arthur Green and Barry W. Holtz.
     p.   cm.
Originally published: New York: Paulist Press, ©1977, in series: The Spiritual Masters.
     Includes bibliographical references.
     ISBN 1-879045-25-7: $14.95
     1. Prayer—Judaism.   2. Hasidism.   3. Contemplation.
     I. Green, Arthur, 1941– .   II. Holtz, Barry W.
     [BM669.Y68   1993]
     296.7'2—dc20   93-25865
                                               , CIP

A JEWISH LIGHTS Classic Reprint
First paperback edition

10 9 8 7 6 5 4 3 2 1

Publishing History

Originally published by Paulist Press, 1977

Schocken Paperback Edition, 1987

Jewish Lights Quality Paperback Edition, with a New Introduction, 1993

Cover illustration by Elaine Greenstein

Manufactured in the United States of America

Published by JEWISH LIGHTS Publishing
A Division of LongHill Partners, Inc.
P.O. Box 237
Sunset Farm Offices, Route 4
Woodstock, Vermont 05091

Tel: (802) 457-4000 *Fax:* (802) 457-4004

For Kathy

who has taught us so much about these texts

and

to the memory of

Esther Schlosberg,

a woman of deep piety and devotion

CONTENTS

INTRODUCTION

I

The world, we are told by the ancient rabbis, stands upon three pillars: Study of Torah, Worship, and Deeds of Compassion. The nature and relative importance of these three pillars of religious life, the intellectual, the devotional, and the activist, have been debated by rabbis and their disciples over the course of many centuries. It was always assumed that the three were deeply intertwined, and that a proper balance among them formed the ideal of Jewish religiosity. No one of these three values was ever allowed to totally supplant the others; nevertheless, there were times and places in the history of Judaism in which one pillar or another seemed to achieve primacy in the minds of pious reflecting Jews.

This is nowhere as clear as in the early period of Hasidism, the great movement of religious revival that brought new spirit to the lives of Jews in the towns and villages of Poland and the Ukraine toward the latter half of the eighteenth century. Here worship, particularly in the form of contemplative prayer, came to be clearly identified by a new group of religious teachers as the central focus of the Jew's religious life. Both the ecstatic outpourings of ordinary people and the highly sophisticated treatments of devotional psychology in the works of early Hasidic masters bear witness to this new and unique emphasis upon the inner life of prayer.

Surely one of the most controversial and often misunderstood movements in Jewish history, Hasidism has undergone several major transformations in the course of its nearly two and a half centuries. Originally seeing itself as a movement of renewal within a wholly traditional, if often spiritually dulled, Jewish community,

Hasidism later took on the task of defending tradition and offering a bastion of resistance to Jews who sought to reject the values of modernity. From that point, early in the nineteenth century, it came to be increasingly identified with the old Jewish way of life, opposed to all change. In our day Hasidism is known as a form of Jewish ultra-Orthodoxy.

But this was hardly the case in the movement's early days. Then the newly emerging circles of teachers and disciples were seen as often unwelcome "newcomers" in the established communities. The values they taught often seemed at odds with the great Jewish traditions of learning and threatening to those who embodied them. Three times, in the course of Hasidism's early spread, rabbis and communal authorities joined in an attempt to destroy the new movement by excommunicating its leaders and those who followed their ways.

What was it that these new masters taught? Their message was simple and in itself wholly traditional, but its challenge to established religion and religious authorities was hardly hidden from view. The early Hasidic masters saw all of Jewish life as "the way of service." Our only task in this world, they taught, is the service of God. Prayer, study, and all of the commandments are to be seen instrumentally: they are the means by which the Jew may fulfill this sacred task. Thus the rabbinic ideal of "study for its own sake" had to be scrutinized and reinterpreted as study for the sake of God, a conscious act of worship. Hasidic authors tirelessly warned their readers against the dangers of robot-like performance of the commandments. Each ritual act must have its way lighted by the glow of inner devotion, else it " has no wings" and cannot ascend to God. Even acts of human kindness, the "Deeds of Compassion" of which the rabbis had spoken, were seen in devotional

4

terms: there is no higher sacred act than that of helping another to discover the presence of God within his or her own soul.

The core of "service" as seen in early Hasidism is the fulfillment of that desire, deeply implanted within each human soul, to return to its original state, to be one with God. Prayer, by its very nature pointing to the intimate relationship between God and soul, becomes the focal point of Hasidic religiosity. The Ba'al Shem Tov (1700-1760), the first great master of the movement, was told by heaven that all his spiritual attainments derived not from any claim to scholarship (as was commonly to be expected in non-Hasidic circles of the time), but rather from the great devotion with which he prayed.

The ecstatic quality of prayer life in early Hasidism has been described in many ways. The Ba'al Shem Tov was said to tremble so greatly in his prayer that bits of grain in a nearby barrel were seen to join him in his trembling. A disciple who touched the master's prayer-garment was so seized with tremors that he had to pray for release. One of the followers was so overcome by ecstasy while preparing for prayer in the ritual bath that he ran from the bathhouse to the adjoining synagogue and danced on the tables without realizing he was not fully dressed. Strange and seemingly inhuman noises, violent movements of the body, even the turning of cartwheels before the Torah, all characterized the devotional climate of some early Hasidic groups. The masters themselves sometimes felt called upon to restore the values of inwardness and silence to a world where unbridled mystical ecstasy was coming to be the order of the day.

What was it about, all this ecstatic frenzy?

5

Prayer was surely not a new discovery for the Jew in the eighteenth century. For nearly two thousand years pious Jews had been reciting their prescribed daily prayers, morning, afternoon, and evening. Private prayers, offered either in Hebrew or in one's spoken tongue, were always considered welcome additions to the fixed liturgy. It had been said of the second-century Rabbi Akiva that if you left him praying in one corner of a room, you were sure to return to find him in the opposite corner, so enthusiastic was his style of worship. Medieval mystics in Germany, France, and Spain had devoted much of their attention to the secrets of inward prayer, turning the recitation of the obligatory liturgy into a setting for the ascent of the soul into ever-higher realms of spiritual existence. Why then all the commotion about prayer at this late date, to the point where the great rabbis of the day were confused and frightened by the forms worship took in the emerging movement?

In order to understand this renewed excitement over prayer, we must realize that Hasidism was, in the truest sense, a revival movement, one that sought to bring new life to old forms that are ever faced with the dangers of petrification and decay. The strength of Judaism has always been its ability to at once preserve and renew its most ancient forms. This is also true with regard to liturgical prayer. The power of liturgy lies largely in its familiarity. The worshiper is enriched by the sense of the words' antiquity: we pray today as did our most ancient ancestors, as our descendants will down to the end of time. So it seems from within the traditional community of prayer. But in this very sameness and constant repetition lies the potential downfall of such prayer, which can degenerate into mere mechanistic recitation. The Ba'al Shem Tov and his followers were acutely aware of this problem. They knew that prayer could only work if it were a constant source for the rediscovery of God's presence throughout the world.

The mystical ecstasy of Hasidism flows from the rediscovery that God is present in all of human life. All things and all moments are vessels that contain the Presence. The prophet's cry "The whole earth is filled with His glory!" and the old Kabbalistic formula "There is no place devoid of Him" became ecstatic watchwords in early Hasidism. Since all of Creation is filled with God's Presence, there is neither place nor moment that cannot become an opening in which one may encounter Him. Hasidism thus teaches that all of life is an extension of the hour of prayer, and that prayer itself is the focal point around which one's entire day is centered.

The followers of the Ba'al Shem Tov were not the first to assert the primacy of prayer in Judaism. For two hundred years before the birth of Hasidism, the mystic teachers who followed in the path of R. Isaac Luria (1534-1572) of Safed had already placed boundless store in the power of man to uplift the fallen world by means of meditative prayer. Lurianic prayer was filled with a kind of urgent and theurgic messianism: by means of an infinitely complex system of theosophical meditations, in which each word and letter was used to address a particular configuration of the divine potencies, prayer could help to bring about the long-awaited redemption of Israel and the world.

Hasidism continued in the Lurianic path, but with two important changes. From the outset, Hasidic piety contained within it an ideal of simplicity. Hasidism may indeed be viewed socially as both the political and spiritual self-assertion of the more modestly educated lower classes against the elitism of the abstrusely learned. Thus the complex contemplative system of the Lurianic Kabbalists, which itself required a great deal of esoteric learning, became intolerable as an ideal. The word spoken with simple wholeness of heart came to be more highly valued than that spoken with deep knowledge of esoteric symbols: the depths of contemplation became open to all who sought truly to enter them. One of the masters explained this change in values by the parable of the keys and the lock. In former times, the mystics had access to a complicated series of keys that could unlock the heart in prayer. We no longer have the keys; all we can do is to smash the lock. The only true prerequisite for such prayer, he said, is a broken heart.

The nature of the redemption to be brought about by prayer and observance of the commandments was also transformed in Hasidism. Largely because of the tragic failure of messianism in the previous century's Sabbatian uprising, the use of prayer as a direct vehicle for historic redemption was downplayed in Hasidic teachings. By means of *devequt*, or intimate attachment to God, one could come to personally transcend all the trials of life in the world, while the external historical situation in face remained unchanged. Redemption *within* this world became the goal. For some Hasidic authors, the *devequt* state as attained by the individual came to replace *tiqqun*, eschatological world-redemption, as the central goal of the religious life.

II

The revolution contained in the Hasidic attitude toward liturgical prayer was perhaps best expressed by R. Pinhas of Korzec. "People think," he said, "that they pray to God. But this is not the case. For prayer itself is of the essence of God!" Prayer is God! The statement seems, at first reading, to be simply an outpouring of ecstasy, the particular meaning of which is difficult to determine. But in fact such a statement is a radical formulation of deeply rooted Hasidic ideas, which form the background of the movement's fascination with prayer.

The human soul, according to Hasidic teaching, is "a part of God above." Religious devotion is caused by the longing of the soul to be reunited with its source, from which it has been separated in the process of human individuation. While souls differ from one another in their inner nature according to their various "roots" or origin above, and while each soul must find its own individual path to *devequt*, all souls can come together in the outpouring process of prayer. Prayer, and particularly the traditional Hebrew prayers of the liturgy, is the vehicle through which the spark of God within the soul may come face to face with the God beyond. Thus prayer itself is the process of *yihud*, the unification of God, always proclaimed by the Kabbalists to be the highest goal of life.

This glorification of the text of prayer is further rooted in the fascination with the mystery of the word, which has always characterized Jewish spirituality. The Biblical account of Creation, in which God creates the world by the mysterious power of speech, plays a formative role in all of later Jewish piety. Augmented by the Kabbalistic creation myth, in which God is said to create through permutations of chains of Hebrew letters, it sets the mysticism of words and letters as one of the central themes of Jewish religious literature. Liturgical prayer recited in the holy tongue, says the Hasidic masters, is but a reordering of the letters, forms them into words of prayer, and brings them back to God. Thus soul and word are undergoing the same process in prayer: they help to carry one another in their shared journey of return to their source in God. In order to pray deeply, a person must truly enter into the letters, until the light of God's Creation, which still dwells within them, is seen.

The centrality of word and letter mysticism in Hasidic thinking is perhaps best illustrated by a well-known story, various versions of which are often quoted in the name of the Hasidic masters. There was once a simple man who used to address God in prayer by saying: "Lord of the World! You know that I have not studied, that I cannot even read the holy words of Your prayerbook. All I remember of that which I learned as child is the alphabet itself. But surely You, Lord, know all the words. So I will give you the letters of the alphabet and You can form the words Yourself." And so he prayed, reciting the letters of the alphabet: *"Aleph, Bet, Gimel..."*

The story, like many Hasidic tales, is not so simple as it first appears. Here two of the great ideals of Hasidic devotion have been combined: the virtue of simplicity and the fascination with the creative powers of the letters, the building blocks of both divine and human speech. The divine energy of Creation formed the universe through the powers of the word; God's speech, in fact, like human speech, may be made accessible if reduced to the constituent letters of the alphabet. In the tale, the simple man has nothing to offer the Lord but the letters. Yet the same is true of the most sophisticated contemplative among the masters. All of us are "simple"; all that we can do in prayer is to return the letters of Creation to their source above.

III

The masters of Hasidic prayer, like most of their predecessors in the Jewish mystical tradition, were hesitant to write down any sort of systematic guide to the ways of contemplation. While they did have a clear sense (particularly in the school of the Maggid of Miedzyrzec) that there were specific ordered steps to be taken that could lead one up the devotional ladder, the composition of such a guide would have been a particular affront to their ideals of spontaneity and wholeness. By what steps in a manual can you guide a person to *hitlahavut*, that state where ecstasy fills the heart like a burning fire? Can any studied method really lead one to know that the soul is nothing but an outpouring of God's ever-flowing light?

Yet despite this lack of systematic introduction, the works of the early Hasidic masters are filled with hints as to the various rungs of inner prayer and how they are to be attained. From these references, scattered throughout early Hasidic literature, a composite picture of their approach to contemplative prayer can be reconstructed. It should be emphasized, however, that the following attempt at systematization is not directly to be found in any single Hasidic source, but is rather culled from the advice of various masters in various situations of spiritual guidance.

There are two types of prayer-state generally described in Hasidic sources. *Qatnut*, the "lesser" or ordinary state in which one generally begins to pray, is opposed to *gadlut*, the "greater" or expanded state of mystical consciousness. Prayer recited while in a state of *qatnu*t may contain within it great devotion; it is generally the simple giving of oneself to God and accepting the divine will. The prayer of *qatnut* may contain both the love of God and awe before God's Presence, the two essential qualities for authentic prayer in Hasidism. In *qatnut*, however, one is not transported beyond the self. Consciousness is not transformed and self-awareness is not transcended. I give myself to God in prayer, but I remain aware of the distinction between giver and receiver of this gift.

The ascent from this state to that of *gadlut* is one of the central themes of Hasidic prayer literature.

While the simple devotions of the *qatnut* state are highly valued, the true goal of the worshiper is to enter that world where "one may come to transcend time," where "distinctions between 'life' and 'death,' 'land' and 'sea,' have lost their meaning." The worshiper seeks to "concentrate so fully on prayer that one no longer is aware of the self...to step outside the body's limits." Rapturous descriptions of the state of *gadlut* abound in Hasidic writings.

The first step in attainment of *gadlut* is the involvement of the entire self in the act of worship. There must be no reservations; you must not hold back any part of your self in prayer. the body is to be involved along with the soul in the act of worship: the rhythmic movement of the body, the sometimes loud outcry of the voice, the training of the eye to the page—all these externals are aids, in the first stages of prayer, to the involvement of the entire self.

As the ecstatic powern of this involvement begins to overwhelm the worshiper, the externals, one by one, are set aside. The body will become still, the shout will become a whisper, and one may put the book aside and see the letters of prayer with the mind's eye alone. This "stripping off of the material world" in the act of prayer corresponds to the essential journey every person must make, according to Hasidic teaching, in the search for truth. The seeker has to shift his eye from external reality, where diversity and multiplicity seem to reign, to the inner truth, where nought but the ever-flowing hiyyut, *or divine life, is real.*

At this point, the winged ascent of the soul and word to the upper worlds begins in earnest. Prayer must ever be accompanied by the love and fear of God, the two emotions Jewish teachers had long seen as the "wings" that allow one's prayer to ascend to God. Each moment of standing at Sinai, when the consuming love of God and the total awe before God's tremendous power were most fully combined. As love and awe accompany the world upward, the letters become liberated from their verbal patterns, and lead the soul back from the "World of Speech" to their higher source in the "World of Thought." Verbal prayer gives way to abstract contemplation, to a liberation of the worshiper's mind from all content other than the attachment to god. First all of one's energies are concentrated on the word as spoken with fullness; the word itself is released and nothing remains with the worshiper but the fullness of heart that, paradoxically, also marks one as an empty vessel ready to receive the light from above. Even the self-conscious feeling of this fullness must be transcended, for "a person who still knows how intensely he is praying has not yet overcome the awareness of self."

This description of the ascent from the verbal to the wholly contemplative state parallels the structure of the cosmos as depicted by the earlier Jewish esoteric tradition. The "World of Speech" is here identified with *shekhinah* (translated throughout this work as "Presence"), the last of the ten divine manifestations around which that tradition centers. *Shekhinah* is the Presence of God in the lower world, the indwelling glory of God that fills all of Creation. It is generally depicted by the mystics in feminine terms; the divinity that inhabits both world and soul longs to be reunited with her transcendent spouse. The "World of Thought" mentioned in these sources refers to *Hokhmah* ("Wisdom,""Sophia"), the highest of the rungs according to Hasidic reckoning. The movement of the worshiper from speech to abstract thought is a journey of ascent through the realms of divine light, from one end of the cosmos to the other.

This emptying of the mind of all content, which Hasidic prayer shares with many other meditative techniques, finally leads to that place *within* God known as the "Nothing" or the realm of Primordial Nothingness. According to Kabbalistic theology, this Nothingness within God is the *ayin* or *nihil* out of which the world was created. All things are rooted in the divine "Nothing." As prayer ascends to God, the creative energy is returned to its source in the One. Creation, however, is viewed in Hasidism as a constant ongoing process: the world is ever pouring forth anew form this state of Nothingness, which lies at the innermost core of being. As the mind is emptied the worshiper stands ready to be filled once again, having returned to that source from which Creation takes place.

Here one has reached the moment of ultimate transformation. In all change and growth, say the masters, the mysterious *ayin* is present. There is an ungraspable instant in the midst of all transformation when that which is about to be transformed is no longer what it had been until that moment, but has not yet emerged as its transformed self; that moment belongs to the *ayin* within God. Since change and transformation are *constant,* however, in fact all moments are moments of contact with the *ayin*, a contact that we are usually too blind to acknowledge. The height of contemplative prayer is seen as such a transforming moment, but one that is marked by a unique blend of awareness and self-transcendence. The worshiper is no longer a separate self, but is fully absorbed, for that moment, in the Nothingness of divinity. That moment of absorption is transforming: the worshiper continues to recite the words of prayer, but is no longer the worshiper who speaks them. Rather it is the Presence who speaks through the one who prays. In that prayerful return to the source, we reach the highest human state, becoming

14

nought but the passive instrument for the ever self-pro-
claiming praise of God.

IV

Any teaching that places such great emphasis on
total concentration in prayer needs to deal with the ques-
tion of distraction. What is a person to do when "alien
thoughts" enter the mind and lead one away from
prayer? Sometimes it seems that the more intensely we
try to concentrate, the more powerful and even sinful
those thoughts become. How is one to be saved from
seeing prayer become a battlefield in which distraction
and self-castigation alternate to keep one far from God?
Surely one who is busily punishing himself for the evil
of wayward thoughts cannot have the joy and wholeness
that are needed for God's service.

It is perhaps in response to this problem that the
Ba'al Shem Tov's thought was most revolutionary. He
spoke against the attempts of his contemporaries to
either do battle with distracting thoughts or to see them
as vanities that should simply be ignored. Just as he
taught that each moment in life may be an opening to the
Presence of God, he taught that each distraction in
prayer may become a ladder by which to ascend to a new
level of devotion. For one who truly believes that all
things are from God and bear the Creator's mark can
make no exception for the fantasies of his or her own
mind! They too are from God, and are sent to us as ways
to God's service. The worshiper must break open the
shell of evil surrounding the distracting thought, find the
root of that thought in God, and join it to prayer. Thus a
person who is distracted by sexual desire during worship
should not seek to drive that desire from the mind, but
rather should come to know that such desire itself is but

15

a fallen spark from the World of Love, which seeks to be uplifted in the ascent of prayer. The thought needs to be "purified in its root," so that the energy animating it can be redeemed and brought back to God. When the Talmud states that a prayer leader who repeats his words and says: "Hear, hear, O Israel!" is to be silenced (probably for fear of dualistic heresy), the Ba'al Shem Tov comments: Why should the poor man be silenced? Perhaps when he said the first "Hear" he was distracted by some other thought, and repeated the word only to pray more devoutly! But that is the very root of dualism! In repeating the word, he is denying the legitimacy of his former prayer; he is denying that God was present in that moment of distraction! And only one who truly knows that God is present in all things, including those thoughts he seeks to flee, can be a leader of prayer.

Behind this matter lies the Ba'al Shem Tov's all-pervading commitment to the full integration of the self, a commitment that was not grasped by all of his disciples. The founder of Hasidism deeply believed that a person torn by inner struggles is not yet ready to come to God. Hence his comments denouncing excessive worry about minor sins. Brooding on our sinfulness, he taught, was merely a trick by the Evil One to keep us far from God. The service of God requires the deepest joy, and such joy cannot be experienced in a divided self. Repent of evil, know that God accepts your penitence in love, and return to serve with joy and wholeness.

V

Because Hasidic literature contains no systematic manual of contemplative prayer, the texts included in the present volume have been culled from many sources. A large number of them have been previously collected in such Hebrew anthologies as *Sefer Ba'al Shem Tov*, by Simeon Mendel Vednik of Gavartchov; *Romemut Ha-Tefillah*, by Shelomo Rosenthal of Warsaw; and *Derekh Hasidim* by Hahman of Cheryn. In all cases, however, the translators have referred to the original sources of material, as indicated in the notes of this volume.

While the notes may be of some interest to students of Hasidism, the primary purpose of the present translation is devotional rather than academic. We offer these texts for the enrichment of the personal religious lives of our readers, for use as readings in the context of worship, and as a source of inspiration to those who seek to uncover the oneness of religious truth behind the garb of various mystical traditions. It is our spiritual situation.

We have taken great care, in translating these texts, not to reinterpret, but rather to allow the Hasidic masters to speak for themselves. Sometimes, however, rearrangement and condensing of the material was required. This is due to the nearly complete lack of concern for literary style on the part of the Hasidic authors and editors. The theoretical literature of Hasidism, in which the prayer instruction texts are often to be found, is poorly edited, often repetitive and sometimes based upon garbled notes in Hebrew summarizing longer sermons that were preached in Yiddish. As such, they at times require some structural rewording when presented in translation, which necessarily involves an attempt to return them, in the translator's mind, to their original oral form and context.

Since this translation was undertaken primarily for devotional purposes, we have sought to avoid use of the third person masculine gender. Such avoidance was not possible in all cases. It is fully the translators' intent that all readers, women as well as men, non-Jews as well as Jews, should have access to the authentic sources of Hasidism.

The sources of this collection are the teachings of the Ba'al Shem Tov, the Maggid Dov Baer of Miedzyrzec, and their immediate disciples, in the latter part of the eighteenth century. Works of such particular Hasidic schools as HaBaD and Bratslav, which differ quite radically both in style and content from these teachings, have not been included.

It should be emphasized that the texts found in this volume did not originate in abstract thought. Many were undoubtedly said to disciples who came to their masters with particular problems in their prayer lives. They belong to moments that can only be recreated in the imagination of the reader. Similarly, this translation is intended for use. Hopefully it will speak to particular moments, touch particular lives. This offering is an attempt to make a modest contribution to the rebirth of religious life, nurtured by the sources of Jewish prayer and the wisdom of its greatest masters.

June, 1993

THE POWER
OF
YOUR PRAYER

What a great wonder that we should be able to
    draw so near to God in prayer.
How many walls there are between man and God!
Even though God fills all the world,
    He is so very hidden!
Yet a single word of prayer can topple all the walls
    and bring you close to God.

When a Jew speaks a word of prayer
in love and awe,
the power of that word gives birth
to God's glory.
The angels call out to God:
"Who is like Your Israel,
a unique people in the world!"
How great is even a single word of such prayer:
it causes all the angels to sing to God!
All the worlds join with the one who serves the Lord.

This is the meaning of "The Song of Songs"—
one who sings a song below can
arouse many songs on high!

Once a wise man was asked: "On what thought do
     you concentrate as you pray?"
He replied: "I bind myself to the Divine Life
     that flows through all of God's creations.
     As I join myself to each
     I seek to bring the life within it back to God."
"Destroyer!" said the other. "How can the world
     exist if you draw out all its life?"
The wise man remained unperturbed:
     "Do you really think I can do all that—
     I who have so little power?"
"But in that case," replied the other,
     "of what value is your prayer?"

The truth is that you must believe
     in the power of your prayer.
The truly wise, who stand before the King in prayer,
     surely can bind themselves to the flow of Life.
But they are not allowed to do so always—
     lest by their uplifting powers
     they do indeed destroy the world.

It is possible to be so humble
    that your very humility
    keeps you far from God.
A humble person may not believe that his own
    prayer
    can cause the Presence
    to flow through all the worlds.
But how then can you believe
    that even angels are nourished
    by your words?

Know the power of your prayer
    and serve your God in fullness!

Why do the prayers of the righteous at times
    seem to go unanswered?

There is a king who has two sons.
Each of them comes to receive his gift
    from the royal table.
The first son appears at his father's doorway,
    and as soon as he is seen, his request is granted.
The father holds this son in low esteem,
    and is annoyed by his presence.
The king orders that the gifts be handed
        to his son at the door
        so that he will not approach the table.

Then the king's
        beloved son appears.
The father takes great pleasure in this son's arrival
        and does not want him to leave too quickly.
For this reason the king delays granting his request,
        hoping that the son will then draw near to him.
As the son comes closer,
        he feels his father's love so deeply
        that he does not hesitate to stretch forth
        his own hand to the royal table.

Both of the sons receive
        what they had sought from their father;
        the portions in themselves are no different.
But the first son receives his gifts in shame,
        seeing that his father stays so far from him.
His brother, however, has come so close to the king
        that he himself can take that which he needs.

Of communal prayer it has been told:

Once in a tropical country, a certain splendid bird,
     more colorful than any that had ever been seen,
     was sighted at the top of the tallest tree.
The bird's plumage contained within it
     all the colors in the world.
But the bird was perched so high
     that no single person
     could ever hope to reach it.

When news of the bird reached the ears of the king,
     he ordered that a number of men
     try to bring the bird to him.
They were to stand on one another's shoulders
     until the highest man could reach the bird
     and bring it to the king.
The men assembled near the tree,
     but while they were standing
     balanced on one another's shoulders,
     some of those near the bottom
     decided to wander off.
As soon as the first man moved,
     the entire chain collapsed,
     injuring several of the men.
Still the bird remained uncaptured.

The men had doubly failed the king.
For even greater than his desire to see the bird
     was his wish to see his people
     so closely joined to one another.

PREPARING
THE
WAY

Faith is the basis of all worship;
    only the truly faithful can pray each day.
And what is the basis of faith?
    "He renews each day the work of Creation."
The faithful one sees
    that every day is a new Creation,
    that all the worlds are new,
    that we ourselves have just been born.
How could we not want to sing
    the praise of the Creator?

If we do not have the faith
    that God creates anew each day,
    prayer becomes an old, unwanted habit.
How difficult it is to say
    the same words day after day!
Thus scripture says: "Cast us not into old age!"—
    may the word never become old for us.

Take special care to guard your tongue
　　before the morning prayer.
Even greeting your fellow, we are told,
　　can be harmful at that hour.
A person who wakes up in the morning is
　　like a new creation.
Begin your day with unkind words,
　　or even trivial matters—
　　　　even though you may later turn to prayer,
　　　　you have not been true to your Creation.
All of your words each day
　　are related to one another.
All of them are rooted
　　in the first words that you speak.

No matter what the season,
    take special care
    to begin your prayer before sunrise.
Most of the service should be completed
    before the sun appears.
The great difference between prayer at dawn
    and prayer recited later in the day
    can hardly be imagined.
Before dawn one can still combat
    the destructive forces of the coming day.
But once the sun is out upon the earth,
    "nothing is hidden from its heat."
Do not consider this a small thing,
    for the Master himself
    took such great care in this matter
    that he would even worship without a quorum
    in order to say his prayers at the proper hour.

A person of spirit may begin to pray
        in awe and trembling,
        saying
        "Who am I, a poor clod of earth,
        to stand before the King of Kings in prayer?"

He speaks only a partial truth.
He does not yet know the higher truth, however—
        the truth that all things,
        even the material world,
        are filled with God's presence.
Indeed he cannot speak the words of prayer—
        better that he remain silent before the Lord.

Thus scripture says:
        "God is in heaven and you are upon the earth;
        do not rush to speak, and let your words be
        few."
As long as you believe that God is only in heaven
        and does not fill the earth—
        let your words be few.
Only when you come to know
        that you too contain His Presence—
        only then can you begin to pray.

How much more pleasing to God is prayer in joy
    than that which is said in sadness and tears!

A poor man begs and weeps
    as he comes before the king;
    he can be dismissed with but a trifle.
But when a noble prince steps forward,
    the king's praises joyfully on his lips,
    and then asks some favor,
    he cannot be treated so lightly.
To him the king grants his greatest gifts—
    a prince must receive a princely portion.

Before you begin to pray,
    decide that you are ready to die
    in that very prayer.
There are some people so intense in their worship,
    who give up so much of their strength to prayer,
    that if not for a miracle they would die
    after uttering only two or three words.
It is only through God's great kindness
    that such people live,
    that their soul does not leave them
    as they are joined to Him in prayer.

There are times when you must prepare yourself
　　　before you can pray.
Reciting Psalms or studying Torah before prayer
　　　may provide the strength you need.
But take care also to avoid giving yourself too fully
　　　to these preparations,
　　　　　lest they consume all your strength
　　　　　and leave no room for prayer itself.

Enter into prayer slowly.
Do not exhaust your strength,
    but proceed step by step.
Even if you are not aroused as your prayer begins,
    give close attention to the words you speak.
As you grow in strength
    and God helps you to draw near,
    you can even say the words more quickly
    and remain in His Presence.

The evil urge has two ways
     of keeping you from prayer;
To each there is an appropriate response.

At times its voice will say to you:
     "Who are you.
     that you dare come into this holy place
     to speak before the Lord?
     How dare you pray—you of unclean lips,
     you who are so filled with sin!"
If you hear these words, reply:
     "See all the good I have done!
     See the way I have kept the Lord's
     commandments,
     how much joy I have brought Him with my
     prayer!"

But even your reply can become an opening
     for the voice of evil.
For the evil urge can also dress itself
     in pride and say:
     "You are the leader of all Israel,
     the greatest of all!
     Surely humility is no virtue
     for one so great as you.
     What a great scholar you are!
     How carefully you fulfill God's commands!"
Know then that this too is the trap
     of the evil one and say:
     "How great are my sins! How empty my
     devotion!
     I have not fulfilled
     even a single one of God's commands!"

There are many people who turn
    the words of prayer into songs.
They even go so far as to plan out
    their worship, saying:
    "Here I will sing this melody; there, another."
They call this the service of God and hope to reach
    states of ecstasy by such song.
They even believe
    that God is pleased by such worship!
What fools they are—
    they walk in darkness
    and have not seen the truth.

A person who is truly at prayer
    must seek to go beyond the material world.
Speak the words simply,
    and devote all your attention
    to the holy letters
    and to the meaning of your prayer.
It is this true devotion
    that will bring you to the love and fear of God—
    and will really set your heart aflame.

MEET HIM
IN THE
WORD

"Make yourself an ark of gopher wood
. . . make a window for the ark
and finish it to a cubit above;
and set the door of the ark in its side;
make it with lower, second and third decks.
. . . Go into the ark,
you and all your household. . . . "

The ark of Noah is the word of prayer.
"Make yourself a window for the ark":
Let the words of prayer
be a window through which
you see to the ends of the earth.

The window is the "light" in the ark
which is the word: Speak the word
in such a way
that the inner light shines through it.

"Make it with lower, second, and third decks."
Each letter contains worlds and souls
and the Presence of God.
As the letters are joined to one another
and form the words of prayer,
all that is within them
rises up to God.
One who joins his soul
to this process
brings all the worlds together in boundless joy.

"Go into the ark,
you and all your household"
—enter into the word
with all your body,
with all your strength.

How does a person come to know God's hidden
    ways?

The stars, which by day are not visible,
    can nevertheless be seen
    by one who uses a proper lens.
The holy letters of prayer form such lenses;
    they may be used as telescopes for seeing into
    the hidden ways of God.
One who has already transcended the self
    and has come to know
    that he is nothing—
    such a person can look so deeply
    into the letters
    that the divine qualities of which they speak
    become real to him.
As one says "the great" during prayer,
    the greatness of God appears
    in those very letters.
Thus one sees the power of God
    in the words "the powerful,"
    the awe of God in the words "the awesome."
The letters themselves have the power
    to draw forth these qualities from above.

It is through the letters
    that the word of God
    may come to dwell with man.

Think that the letters of prayer
    are the garments of God.
What a joy to be making a garment
    for the greatest of kings!
Enter into every letter with all your strength.
God dwells within each letter;
    as you enter it, you become one with Him.

See your prayer as arousing the letters
    through which heaven and earth
    and all living things were created.
The letters are the life of all;
    when you pray through them,
    all Creation joins with you in prayer.
All that is around you can be uplifted;
    even the song of a passing bird
    may enter into such a prayer.

Put all your strength into the words,
  proceeding from letter to letter
  with such concentration
  that you lose awareness of your bodily self.
It will then seem that the letters themselves
  are flowing into one another.
This uniting of the letters is one's greatest joy.
If joy is felt as two human bodies come together,
  how much greater must be the joy
  of this union in spirit!

Know that each word of prayer is a complete self.
If all of your strength is not in it,
    it is born incomplete,
    like one lacking a limb.

When you focus all your thought
        on the power of the words,
        you may begin to see the sparks of light
        that shine within them.
The sacred letters are the chambers
        into which God pours His flowing light.
The lights within each letter, as they touch,
        ignite one another,
        and new lights are born.

It is of this the Psalmist says:
        "Light is sown for the righteous,
        and joy for the upright in heart."

"With the Lord your God"

God is present in the words of Torah.
Enter into the words,
    speaking them with all your strength.
Your soul will then meet God in the word—
    that soul which is itself a part of God above.

This is the true union of the Holy One, blessed be
    He,
    and His Presence, of which the mystics speak.
"With the Lord your God"—with the Lord, *your*
    God—
    the Presence within you, *your* God,
    is joined together with "the Lord"—
    its eternal source.

If prayer is pure and untainted,
  surely that holy breath
  that rises from your lips
  will join with the breath of heaven
  that is always flowing
  into you from above.
Thus our masters have taught the verse
  "Every breath shall praise Him":
  with every single breath that you breathe,
  He is praised.
As the breath leaves you, it ascends to God,
  and then it returns to you from above.
Thus that part of God
  which is within you
  is reunited with its source.

The purpose of all prayer is to uplift the words,
    to return them to their source above.
The world was created
    by the downward flow of letters:
Our task is to form those letters into words
    and take them back to God.
If you come to know this dual process,
    your prayer may be joined
    to the constant flow of Creation—
    word to word, voice to voice,
    breath to breath, thought to thought.

The words fly upward and come before Him.
As God turns to look at the ascending word,
    life flows through all the worlds
    and prayer receives its answer.
All this happens in an instant
    and all this happens continually;
Time has no meaning in the sight of God.
The divine spring is ever-flowing;
    make yourself into a
    channel
    to receive the waters from above.

When a person prays in an ordinary way,
    the words of prayer have no life of their own.
It is only the name of God appearing in their midst
    that gives them life.
Thus when you recite the words:
    "Blessed art Thou, O Lord . . . , "
    life does not enter the words
    until the word "Lord" is uttered.

But when a true master of prayer recites the words
    every word is a name of God.
"Blessed" is a name, "Thou" is a name. . . .

Do not think that the words of prayer
    as you say them
    go up to God.
It is not the words themselves that ascend;
    it is rather the burning desire of your heart
    that rises like smoke toward heaven.
If your prayer consists only of words and letters,
    and does not contain your heart's desire—
    how can it rise up to God?

BEYOND
THE WALLS
OF SELF

"Go out of the ark,
   you and your wife and your children."

Take *yourself* out of the words of your prayer.
Let your prayer not be for yourself
   or for your household,
   but only for the sake of God and His Presence.

A person should be so absorbed in prayer
    that he is no longer
    aware of his own self.
There is nothing for him but the flow of Life;
    all his thoughts are with God.
He who still knows how intensely he is praying
    has not yet overcome the bonds of self.

You must forget yourself in prayer.
Think of yourself as nothing
    and pray only for the sake of God.
In such prayer you may come to transcend time,
    entering the highest realms
    of the World of Thought.
There all things are as one;
Distinctions between ''life'' and ''death,''
    ''land'' and ''sea,''
    have lost their meaning.
But none of this can happen
    as long as you remain attached
    to the reality of the material world.
Here you are bound to the distinctions
    between good and evil
    that emerge only in the lower realms of God.
How can one who remains attached to his own self
    go beyond time to the world where all is one?

The human body is always finite;
It is the spirit that is boundless.
Before you begin to pray,
    cast aside that which limits you
    and enter the endless world of Nothing.
In prayer turn to God alone
    and have no thoughts of yourself at all.
Nothing but God exists for you;
    you yourself have ceased to be.
The true redemption of the soul can only happen
    as you step outside the body's limits.

In prayer seek to make yourself into a vessel
    for God's Presence.
God, however, is without limit;
"Endless" is His name.
How can any finite vessel hope to contain
    the endless God?
Therefore, see yourself as nothing:
    only one who is nothing
    can contain the fulness
    of the Presence.

As long as you can still say the words
    "Blessed art Thou"
    by your own will,
    know that you have not yet reached
    the deeper levels of prayer.
Be so stripped of selfhood that you have
    neither the awareness
    nor the power
    to say a single word on your own.

Why are we told to recite the verse
        "O Lord, open my lips
        and let my mouth declare Your praise"
        before our most sacred prayer?
Like banks to a river,
        lips form the outer edges of human speech.
We pray that God may release us from those limits,
        so that our mouths may declare
        His endless praise.

As a person begins to pray, reciting the words:
"O Lord, open my lips
and let my mouth declare Your praise,"
the Presence of God comes into him.
Then it is the Presence herself
who commands his voice;
it is she who speaks the words *through* him.
One who knows in faith
that all this happens within him
will be overcome with trembling
and with awe.

There are times when the love of God
      burns so powerfully within your heart
      that the words of prayer seem to rush forth,
      quickly and without deliberation.
At such times it is not you yourself who speak;
      rather it is *through* you
      that the words are spoken.

When you speak, think that the World of Speech is
    at work within you,
    for without that presence,
    you would not be able to speak at all.
Similarly, you would not think at all were it not
    for the World of Thought within you.
A person is like a ram's horn;
    the only sound you make is
    that which is blown through you.
Were there no one blowing into the horn,
    there would be no sound at all.

There are two rungs of service
　　　　that a person can come to know.
The first is called *Qatnut*, "the lesser service."
In this state you may know
　　　　that there are many heavens encircling you,
　　　　that the earth on which you stand is
　　　　but a tiny point,
　　　　and that all the world is nothing
　　　　before the Endless God—
　　　　but even knowing all these things,
　　　　you yourself cannot ascend.
This is still the "lesser" service.
It is of this state the prophet says:
　　　　"from afar God appears to me."

But when you serve in *Gadlut*, "the greater service,"
　　　　you take hold of yourself with all your strength
　　　　and your mind soars upward,
　　　　breaking through the heavens all at once,
　　　　rising higher,
　　　　higher than the angels.

There are times when you are praying
    in an ordinary state of mind
    and you feel that you cannot draw near to God.
But then in an instant
    the light of your soul will be kindled
    and you will go up to the highest worlds.

You are like one who has been given a ladder:
The light that shines in you is a gift from above.

PRAYER
FOR THE
SAKE OF HEAVEN

All of your prayers should be
for the sake of the Presence,
who herself is called prayer.
Each of your needs is only a reflection
of some lack in the Presence.
Pray for her fulfillment,
not merely your own.
As you bring oneness to the upper worlds
and restore that which is lacking above,
your own needs too will be fulfilled.

All the wonders that the Master performed—
healing the sick and dying,
opening the eyes of the blind,
restoring the wellsprings gone dry,
helping the barren to conceive,
great miracles that the world had not seen
since the days of Hanina ben Dosa—
All this came about because our Master thought
only of that which was lacking above.

"There is no place without Him"—
every deed you do is a dwelling-place for
God.

Maimonides says in his credo:
    "One should pray to Him alone;
    to no one else should he pray."
But the text can also be read:
    "One should pray *for* Him alone;
    for nothing else should he pray."
The purpose of Creation is only that we pray for
    God.
Material things, this world—
    such nonsense is not worthy of prayer.

The Psalmist says:
   "A prayer of a poor man"—
But the text may also read:
   "A prayer *to* a poor man!"

Though the treasure houses of the king are full,
   they are managed by the king's officials.
Having nothing to do with all his treasures,
   the king himself is like a poor man.

One who comes in search of treasure
   will never see the King.
Only one who seeks no riches,
   who prays as to a poor man,
      can come before the King Himself.

"Do not be like those who serve the master
        in order to receive a reward.
        Be rather like those who serve the master
        not in order to receive a reward."
But another version of this text reads:
        " . . . serve the master
        in order *not* to receive a reward!"
Both versions are correct, but the latter
        speaks of a higher rung of service.

The first version surely speaks
        of a proper kind of prayer,
        one in which the worshiper
        directs his thoughts only
        to the needs of God.
It matters little to him
        whether his own personal petition
        is granted or denied.
All of this servant's deeds
        are for the sake of heaven.

But there is yet a higher rung,
        of which the second version speaks.
There is a man who lives with a burning desire
        to speak with the king.
The king has issued a decree that anyone
        who comes forward with a petition
        shall have his wish granted.
This man, however, longs only
        to stand before the king
        and speak with him always.
In him the king's decree arouses only fear:

whatever he asks, the king will grant,
and no longer will he be able to speak with him!
He would rather his petition not be granted,
so that he might have reason always
to return to the presence of the king.
This man serves "in order
not to receive a reward."

This is the meaning of:
"a prayer of a poor man who is faint,
pouring forth his words before the Lord."
This poor man seeks nothing more in prayer
than that his words pour forth before the Lord.

The liturgy prescribes that
     the Prayer of Love must be recited
     before the Proclamation of God's Oneness.
The Master was told that the Messiah has not come
     because people do not
     devote themselves sufficiently to this prayer.
These words of love are the kisses
     that precede sexual union,
     awakening desire in the Presence
     so that her child, compassion,
     might come forth.

Do not rush through your weekday prayers thinking:
    "on the Sabbath I will pray with spirit."
In such prayer you would be like the king's servant
    who seems deeply attached to his tasks
    only as long as the king
    stands before him, but loses his devotion
    when the king is not in view.
This is not a faithful servant.

If you truly want to serve, know in faith
    that there is no good
    for you in life without the King.
Serve always as you do
    when the King stands before you.

To those beset by suffering,
        the following has been told:

There was a man who had a young child.
At times the father sought to frighten the boy.
He would dress up in strange clothing
        so that his son would not know him.
At first the child was frightened,
        but as time passed he came to know
        that this too was his father.
Then he would call out "Father!"
        and the father, filled with compassion,
        would take off the disguise
        and reveal himself to his son.

So it is with those who suffer.
When they come to understand
        that it is God Himself
        who is the source of their pain,
        they can then begin to call out to Him.
But those who do not see that all is from God
        and seek their cure elsewhere—
        these will never find true healing.

IN HIS PRESENCE

"Pour out your heart like water
    in the Presence of the Lord."

On the second day of Creation,
    God separated the upper and lower waters.
At the moment of their separation, we are told,
    the lower waters cried out:
        "We too long to be near our Creator!"

So it is with the soul:
    it too once dwelt in the upper realms,
    near to God,
    and has fallen to the lowest depths.
Like the lower waters of Creation,
    it cries out to return to God.
"Pour out your heart like the waters,"
    says the Psalmist,
    longing again to be
    "in the Presence of the Lord."

We are told that God's name as it is spoken means
     that He is Lord of all.
But the Name as written is that of God beyond:
     He who was and is and will be,
     the source of life for all the worlds.
The very letters of this Name are themselves
     the source of life.

When those of understanding heart begin to pray
     and come upon the Name,
     they see all this before them.
Can there be a greater joy than speaking face to face
     with the Eternal King, the life of every soul?
Of such moments scripture says:
     "Let Him kiss me with the kisses of His
     mouth."

Prayer is union with the Divine Presence.
Just as two people will move their bodies
>back and forth as they begin the act of love,
>so must a person accompany
>the beginning of prayer
>with the rhythmic swaying of the body.
But as one reaches the heights of union
>with the Presence,
>the movement of the body ceases.

Be joyful always.
Know that God's Presence is with you,
    that you are looking directly at your Creator
    and your Creator at you.
Know that the Creator can do all that He desires:
    that in an instant
    He could destroy all the worlds,
    and in an instant renew them.
In Him are rooted all powers, both good and
    harmful;
His flowing life is everywhere.
Only Him do I trust!
Only Him do I fear!

What is *devequt*, or attachment to God,
      of which the masters speak?

Some say that it is a holding fast to each word—
      attachment to each word is so great
      that one cannot bear to part with it.

But others say that this attachment comes to one
      who truly fulfills God's commands—
      making the body a throne for the mind,
      the mind a throne for the spirit,
      and the spirit a throne for the soul.
Then the soul too becomes a throne
      for the light of the Presence
      that rests upon him.
The light spreads forth around him,
      and he, at the center of that light,
      trembles in his joy.

"When God is seated upon His throne,
    a fire of silence falls upon
    the heavenly beings."

When a person says the words of prayer
    so that they become a throne for God
    an awesome silent fire takes hold of him.
Then he knows not where he is;
    he cannot see, he cannot hear.
All this happens in the flash of an instant—
    as he ascends beyond the world of time.

It is possible to pray in such a way
that no other person
can know of your devotion.
Though you make no movement of your body,
your soul is all aflame within you,
And when you cry out in the ecstasy of that
moment—
your cry will be a whisper.

There are times when a person's body
  may remain completely still
  while the soul serves God in silent prayer.
In such moments your prayer may be filled
  with a burning and awesome love,
  though one who sees you
  might never guess the depth
  of your inner service.
Only those who are already at one with God
  may attain this prayer
  of inner flame and outer stillness.
Such worship has greater power
  than devotion which can be seen by others.
The "shells" of evil which feed upon wayward
  prayers
  cannot reach this silent prayer,
  for it is deeply hidden within the self.

Learn to pray quietly;
    even God's praises should be recited
    in a low voice.
Your shouts should be whispers.
But even so, say the words with all your strength,
    as it is written:
        "All my bones shall say: 'O Lord, who is like
        You!'"
Those who truly cleave to God—
    their outcry is a whisper.

A person may come to sense two kinds of movement
       taking place within him during prayer.
At times you may feel the left hand of God
       pushing you away;
       at other times God's right hand draws you near.
But even as you are pushed away,
       know still
       that this is only for the sake of your return.
Even as you feel
       the might of God's left hand upon you,
       see that it is God Himself
       who touches you.
This too accept in love,
       and, trembling, kiss the hand that pushes you—
       for in that very moment,
       the right hand awaits your coming near.

THOUGHTS
THAT LEAD
ASTRAY

Even the distracting thoughts
　　that confound you during prayer
　　may be a good sign.

In a palace surrounded by many walls
　　there lives a king.
At each entrance there is a guard posted,
　　to keep people from approaching.
If the petitioner who comes to see the king
　　is a man of no importance,
　　the guards will not bother with him.
They will allow him to enter the palace undisturbed.
In any case they know
　　that the king will pay him no attention.
But how different it is
　　when a respected noble of the kingdom
　　tries to come before the king,
　　one with a request that could endanger
　　the position of the guards themselves.
Then they try to put him off
　　in whatever way they can,
　　telling him to leave and come back some other
　　time.
How they try to keep him from the king—
　　for surely his words would be accepted
　　by their master!

All this is said of prayer.
When you realize that
　　you are being kept away from the king,
　　gather up all your strength
　　and cry out in anguish:
　　"Father, save me!"
God longs to hear His people's prayer—
　　one cry can open all the gates.

This parable is told of prayer:

Once there was a road
　　that was known to be very dangerous,
　　for it passed through a forest that was filled
　　with highwaymen and robbers.
These thieves would lie in wait
　　for a traveller to come through the forest.
As he passed near them,
　　they would pour out of their hideouts
　　and fly at the throat of their victim,
　　to rob for profit or simply to destroy.
Those who travelled this road were known
　　to pass quickly through the forest,
　　hoping to give the thieves
　　no chance to fall upon them.

It happened that two men
　　came to travel the way together.
One of them was very drunk, while the other was
　　sober.
As they walked through the forest,
　　the sober man pressed forward quickly
　　until he had passed through the wood unharmed.
His drunken friend, however, lumbered slowly
　　along,
　　step after heavy step.
The murderers attacked him,
　　beating him and covering his body
　　with wounds and bruises.
But because of his drunkenness,
　　he felt nothing at all.

At the far edge of the forest the two men met.
The sober man was shocked at his friend's condition

and asked him how he had managed
to survive the attack.
The drunk was no less shocked
at his companion's questions,
for he believed nothing had happened to him at
all.
Finally his friend brought him a looking-glass,
and showed him how battered and bruised he
was,
and the bloodstains that covered his clothes.
All this baffled the drunk;
He remembered nothing at all.

When a distracting thought comes to you in prayer,
    hold fast to God and break through
    to redeem the sacred spark
    that dwells within that thought.

The son of a rich man was once taken captive
    and held for ransom.
The father did nothing for his son,
    but merely sat at home, counting out his
    fortune.
Suddenly he saw his son before him;
The boy cried out:
    "Father! What are you doing?
    You have all this money—
    stop counting and redeem your son!"

"If I am not for myself, who is for me?
    If I am only for myself, what am I?"

A person at prayer should go beyond his own self,
    no longer feeling any attachment
    to the material world.
As long as I "*am* for myself,"
    I cannot go beyond distraction.
Only when I no longer know my own existence
    will I be freed from all such thoughts.
When I have reached that rung of prayer,
    "who *is* for me?"—
    if I am no longer aware of my own self,
    what distracting thought can disturb me?

"*If I am only for myself*"–
    if I do think of myself
    as existing in this world,
    then I am indeed nothing.
In that case, "*what am I?*"—
    what am I worth and of what value is my
    service?
Distracting thoughts will so confound me
    that I will be as nothing,
    unable to stand before Him.

And what is our existence but the service of God?

"No man shall go up with you;
No man shall be seen upon that mountain."

As you stand before God in prayer,
     you should feel that you stand alone—
     in all the world only you and God exist.
Then there can be no distractions;
Nothing can disturb such prayer.

Do not laugh at one who moves his body,
    even violently, during prayer.
A person drowning in a river
    makes all kinds of motions
    to try to save himself.
This is not a time for others to laugh.

Prayer is never repeated:
    the quality of each day's prayer
    is unlike that of any other.
This is the inner meaning of the Mishnah's words:
    "One whose prayer is rigid
    prays without supplication."
This can be seen even in the thoughts
    that distract us from true prayer;
They too are different every day.
Each day and its prayer,
    each day and its distractions—
    until Messiah comes.

THE WAY
OF THE
SIMPLE

The tale is told of a king who one day discovered
    that the great seal of his kingdom was missing.
You cannot imagine
    how terrible was this loss for him,
    for whoever found the seal could issue decrees
    in the king's own name.
And even if no one ever did find it,
    what a disgrace
    that the king's great seal should be
    lying in the dust!
The king was saddened by his loss,
    and his sorrow was felt
    by all the royal household.
All joined in the search—
    but because they sought so carefully
    and longed so greatly to find the seal,
    they passed it by.
Then a poor farmer happened along and,
    simply glancing about,
    he came upon the seal.
Though he knew nothing of the importance of his
    find,
    this simple farmer brought the king great joy.
The farmer also rejoiced,
    still understanding little of what he had done,
    but saying to himself:
    "The king's own seal! The king's own seal!"

The parable is not explained.

Through everything you see,
    become aware of the divine.
If you encounter love, remember the love of God.
If you experience fear, think of the fear of God.
And even in the bathroom, you should think—
    "here I am separating bad from good,
    and the good will remain for His service!"

One who reads the words of prayer with great
    devotion
        may come to see the lights within the letters,
        even though one does not understand
        the meaning of the words one speaks.
Such prayer has great power;
Mistakes in reading are of no importance.

A father has a young child whom he greatly loves.
Even though the child has hardly learned to speak,
    his father takes pleasure
        in listening to his words.

A parable is told of a man who wants to eat
    and who feels a great hunger
    for a certain food.
He then sees the very food he wants
    in a place high above him,
    beyond his reach.
In his hunger he begins to imagine
    that he is eating the food
    that he desires.
But what has he gained by such imaginings?
He is only more hungry than before.

The same is true of those who try to reach
    for the highest esoteric meaning of each prayer.
They are far from such things;
    their minds simply cannot reach
    the heights for which they strive.
What good does it do them?

Better not to reach for things beyond your grasp.

The mystics have discovered many levels of meaning
    in each word of prayer.
No one person can know them all.
One who tries to meditate
    on the hidden meanings of prayer
    can only reach those secrets which are known to
    him.

But if in prayer you join
    your whole self to every word,
    all the secret meanings
    enter the word of their own accord.
Every letter becomes a complete world.
What a great thing you do!
Worlds above are awakened by your prayer.
Thus should your prayer be fire—
    for every letter awakens worlds above.

To one who moved his body violently in prayer,
    it was told:

A candle wick may be made of cotton or of flax.
With one sort of wick
    the candle makes a great deal of noise
    as it burns,
    while the other sort of candle burns in silence.
Does the silent candle give less light?

The slightest movement of your little toe,
    if it is done in truth,
    may be sufficient.

Sometimes while at prayer you may feel
    that you cannot enter
    the upper world at all.
Your mind remains below and you think:
    "The whole *earth* is full of His glory."
But really you are nearer to God than you know.
At such times you are like a child
    who has just begun to understand
    how close to God he is.
Even though your mind cannot yet transcend this
    world,
    God is with you in your prayer.

How does so lowly a creature as man
    dare to come before God
    three times each day
    to seek fulfillment of his needs?

There was a king who had a garden
    in which he took great pride.
He hired a certain man to care for it:
    to plant, to trim, to cultivate the earth.
Now that gardener needed sustenance for himself
    and various supplies to tend the royal garden.
Should he be ashamed to come before the king
    each day and seek that which he needs?
It is for the king himself that he is working!

But such is not the case for a lazy worker,
    one who does nothing for the garden,
    but only takes what is given him
    to satisfy his gluttonous desires.
How can he dare to come again before the king and
    say:
    "Give me what I want"?

How do we have the audacity
      to ask for God's compassion?
It is only because God's love for us is like
      the love of a father for his child.
Even if the child pulls at his beard,
      a father's love is not diminished.

A parable of prayer:

A father and his son, travelling together in a wagon,
    came to the edge of a forest.
Some bushes, thick with berries,
    caught the child's eye.
"Father," he asked, "may we stop awhile
    so that I can pick some berries?"
The father was anxious to complete his journey,
    but he did not have it in his heart
    to refuse the boy's request.
The wagon was called to a halt,
    and the son alighted to pick the berries.

After a while,
    the father wanted to continue on his way.
But his son had become so engrossed in
    berry-picking
    that he could not bring himself
    to leave the forest.
"Son!" cried the father, "we cannot stay here all
    day!
    We must continue our journey!"

Even his father's pleas were not enough
    to lure the boy away.
What could the father do?
Surely he loved his son no less
    for acting so childishly.
He would not think of leaving him behind—
    but he really did have to get going
    on his journey.

Finally he called out:
    "You may pick your berries for a while longer,

but be sure that you are still able to find me,
for I shall start moving slowly along the road.
As you work, call out 'Father! Father!'
every few minutes, and I shall answer you.
As long as you can hear my voice,
know that I am still nearby.
But as soon as you can no longer hear my answer,
know that you are lost,
and run with all your strength to find me!''

AFTER
THE HOUR
OF
PRAYER

A person at prayer is like a bed of coals,
As long as a single spark remains,
 a great fire can again be kindled.
But without that spark there can be no fire.

Always remain attached to God,
 even in those times
 when you feel unable to ascend to Him.
You must preserve that single spark—
 lest the fire of your soul be extinguished.

Take special care of what you do in the moments
    immediately after prayer.
The spirit of your worship may remain with you
    and affect your thoughts and deeds.
One who prayed with great fear of heaven
    may see awe turn to anger.
One whose prayer was an outpouring of love
    may be overwhelmed by unwanted
    passion.
In order to avoid such pitfalls,
    it is best after prayer
    to begin at once your work or study.

These words require careful thought,
    but their implications are best
    not committed to writing.

The hour of formal prayer is not the only time
    when you may seek to bind yourself to God.
In doing so outside the hour of prayer,
    however,
    take special care
    that no one else be near you
    as you ascend to the higher worlds.
Even the chirping of birds could disturb you;
Even the unspoken thought of another person
    could bring you back to earth.

When you seek to be alone with God,
    have at least one companion with
    you.
Alone one is in danger.
When two are in the same room,
    each of them may turn to God separately.
When you are more experienced
    you may sometimes meditate alone in a room—
    But surely someone else should be
    in the same house with you.

There are times when you are not at prayer,
	but nevertheless you can feel close to God.
Your mind can ascend even above the heavens.

And there are also times,
	in the very midst of prayer,
	when you find yourself unable to ascend.
At such times stand where you are
	and serve with love.

A
FINAL
PARABLE

This parable is told:

There was once a musician,
    well-known for the great beauty
    of his music, who came to play before the king.
One particular melody was so loved by the king
    that he ordered the musician
    to play it for him several times each day.
And so it was.
After a time, however,
    the musician began to weary of the tune;
    no longer could he play it with the same passion
    and excitement as before.

The king, to rekindle his musician's love
    for this favorite tune,
    ordered that a man be brought in from the
    market,
    one who had never heard the tune before.
Seeing someone who had never heard him play,
    the musician's vigor was renewed,
    and he played the tune in all its beauty,
Thus the king ordered a new man brought each day.

After some time, the king sought other counsel,
    for to find a new audience each day
    was not an easy matter.
It was decided that the musician should be blinded,
    so that he never see a human form again.
Now the blind musician sat before the king,
    and whenever the king sought
    to hear his favorite tune
    he would simply say:
    "Here comes someone new,
    one who has never heard you play before!"

118

And the musician would play his tune
  with the greatest joy.

The parable is not explained.

NOTES

The number preceding each of the following notes refers to the page number within this book.

Citations in these notes are in accord with Hebrew works listed. Numbers refer to folio side and column in accord with pagination of traditional Hebrew works.

20   Liqqutim Yeqarim 2b.

21   Maggid Devaraw Le-Ya'aqov 27a.

22   Or Ha-Me'ir 5:31c. This translation is a free rendition, hoping to recapture the spirit of this dialogue. For a more literal translation and discussion of the passage, cf. Scholem's *The Messianic Idea in Judaism*, p. 242.

23   Toledot Ya'aqov Yosef 172c.

24   Tif'eret 'Uzi'el 134. Based on a parable attributed to Rabbi Akiba in Jerusalem Talmud Ta'anit 3:4.

25   Or Ha-Hokhmah 4:31b-32a.

28   Degel Maḥaneh Ephraim 234-5. The two quotations are from the daily liturgy and from Psalm 71:9.

29   Liqqutim Yeqarim 12a; Keter Shem Tov 37a.

30   Ẓawa'at RIVaSH 3a. Kabbalists placed great emphasis upon the sacred quality of the hours of dawn and dusk as proper times for prayer. Cf. Magen Avraham to Shulḥan 'Arukh, Oraḥ Ḥayyim 1:1. According to the Zohar (1:178a), the central *'Amidah* prayer, which on weekdays contains a series of petitions, should be recited immediately *after* the rising of the sun, as the moments

preceding sunrise are too intimate to be interrupted by mere petition.

31 Hit'orerut Ha-Tefillah 3a-b. The quotation is from Ecclesiastes 5:1.

32 Zawa'at RIVaSH 13a.

33 Zawa'at RIVaSH 4b-5a, 6b-7a; Liqqutim Yeqarim 1a; Siftey Zaddiqim 29c. The present translation is a conflate of these several versions.

34 Toledot Ya'aqov Yosef 83a.

35 Zawa'at RIVaSH 4a-b. There are times, however, when the masters recommend that the worshiper rush quickly through the words of prayer—perhaps so that distractions will have no chance to grab hold. Cf. p. 91 below.

36 Hit'orerut Ha-Tefillah 7b.

37 Pitgamin Qaddishin 17a. While the importance of music in Hasidism is well-known, and the wordless *niggun* became a characteristic Hasidic form of contemplation, the masters opposed the conversion of the liturgy into a platform for the "artistic" cantor.

40 A series of interpretations of Genesis 6:14ff., based on the dual meaning of the word *tevah*, the Biblical term for "ark", which can also mean "word" in Rabbinic Hebrew.

Or Ha-Me'ir 2:11b.

Toledot Yizhaq 3a.

Zawa'at RIVaSH 8b. Another version in Degel Mahaneh Ephraim 9b.

Zawa'at RIVaSH 8b; Hesed Le-Avraham 53a.

41 Shemu'ah Tovah 73b. The phrase "the great, the pow-

erful, and the awesome" is found in the first blessing of
the daily 'Amidah prayer, derived in turn from Deut.
10:17. According to the Kabbalists, each of these adjec-
tives represents a particular aspect of the Divine Self:
"the great" is divine love (ḥesed), "the powerful" is
divine judgement (din), and "the awesome" is divine
majesty (tif'eret) which mediates between the two
others.

42   Zawa'at RIVaSH 13a.

43   Darkhey Zedeq 6b, no. 39. The creation of the universe
     by means of the letters of the Hebrew alphabet is a
     well-known motif in Jewish literature.

44   Keter Shem Tov 72b.

45   Liqqutim Yeqarim 2a; Zawa'at RIVaSH 4b.

46   Keter Shem Tov 47b, quoting Psalm 97:11.

47   Or Ha-Emet 36b. This is the heart of mystical union as
     portrayed in Hasidism: the soul of man is itself a part of
     God, cut off from its source by the veil (or illusion, to
     some schools) of separate existence. In prayer and con-
     templation, that of God which dwells within the soul,
     "your" God in this passage, is united with God beyond.
     The passage from Deut. 10:12 is taken as though it read:
     "with the Lord—your God".

48   Liqqutim Yeqarim 12a. Based on the re-reading of
     Psalm 150:6 found in Midrash Bereshit Rabbah 14:9 (ed.
     Theodor p. 134).

49   Liqqutim Yeqarim 10a; Or Torah 58b-59a.

50   Maggid Devaraw Le-Ya'aqov 17a.

51   Or Ha-Me'ir 3:16c.

54   Torey Zahav 5:4. Cf. the note to p. 40 above.

55   Or Ha-Emet 2b.

123

56 Maggid Devaraw Le-Ya'aqov 69a. The term "World of Thought" is a common Hasidic designation for the deepest and most hidden of the divine manifestations (*Sefirot*). The "World of Thought" comes to be revealed in the "World of Speech", the lowest of the ten manifestations, also called *Shekhinah* ("Presence"), in a way parallel to the revelation of a person's deepest thoughts in the words he speaks. The upper Sefirotic realm, that of *Hokhmah* or Thought, is one of complete unity, where distinctions of both individual identity and moral judgement have not yet come to be.

57 Shemu'ah Tovah 79b-80a.

58 Maggid Devaraw Le-Ya'aqov 69a. "Endless" here is used to translate *Eyn Sof*, the Kabbalistic term for the hidden Godhead. It literally means "without end".

59 'Avodat Yisra'el 98b. The author explains that one's ability to go on with reciting the liturgy at such moments surely must be a divine gift.

60 Shemu'ah Tovah 80a. The comment is on the thrice-daily recitation of Psalm 51:17 as an introduction to the *'Amidah* prayer. The Hebrew word *safah* may mean either "lip" or "riverbank". See also the following text.

61 Maggid Davaraw Le-Ya'aqov 14a.

62 Zawa'at RIVaSH 4b; Keter Shem Tov 38b. The latter source describes such a devotee as one "drunk" with prayer. The Zawa'at RIVaSH version, used in this translation, deletes the word *shikor*. Hasidim, who were accused by their enemies of excessive drinking, may have chosen to censor such a positive reference to spiritual inebriation in their early literature.

63 Maggid Devaraw Le-Ya'aqov 68b. The ram's horn (*shofar*) is used in Jewish liturgy, especially on the New Year, recalling the ram who replaced Isaac on the altar.

64 Ẓawa'at RIVaSH 18a. The respective values placed on the two prayer states should not be oversimplified: while *gadlut* is generally taken to be the ideal state for worship, statements in praise of the simple devotion of *qatnut* are by no means lacking in Hasidic literature. Cf. below, p. 106 and p. 115.

65 Liqqutim Yeqarim 3d.

68 Hekhal Berakhah 4:82a. "Prayer" as a name for the Shekhinah is found in earlier mystical literature. Cf. Cordovero, *Pardes Rimmonim* (ed. Munkacs) v.2, p. 45. Ḥanina ben Dosa was a great wonderworker and master of prayer in the first century.

69 Sefer Ba'al Shem Tov, parashat Noah, n.118. Quoted in the name of Aaron of Kaidanow, presumably by oral tradition.

70 Toledot Ya'aqov Yosef 169b. A comment on Psalm 102:1. It is made obvious in the context that neither the king nor his beloved servant will want for lack of treasures—but such treasures are not a worthy object of prayer.

71 Degel Maḥaneh Ephraim 253. The passage is a comment on the saying of Antigonus of Sokho in Avot 1:3. On the two versions in that source cf. the commentary of R. Jonah Gerondi ad loc.

73 Toledot Ya'aqov Yosef 38d. The reference is to the prayer *ahavat 'olam* ("Eternal Love") which immediately precedes the recitation of the *shema'*, the proclamation of God's unity which is the center of Jewish worship.

74 Ẓawa'at RIVaSH 10a,

75 Oraḥ Le-Ḥayyim 386b. Hasidic teachings claim that everything, including suffering and evil, comes from

God. While on one level this recognition is the basis for even the beginning of a prayer-life, final acceptance of it can be seen only as prayer's most ultimate goal.

78 Hit'orerut Ha-Tefillah 4a. Based on a Midrashic source; cf. Jellinek's *Bet ha-Midrash* 1:63 (*Midrash 'Aseret ha-Dibrot*).

79 Ketonet Passim 43b. Based on an explanation of *Tur Orah Hayyim* 5 which discusses the difference in meaning between the ineffable name YHWH and the reading *adonai*, by which the name is pronounced in the liturgy.

80 Zawa'at RIVaSH 7b. The sexual metaphor is often applied to prayer in early Hasidic literature. The passage in Toledot Ya'aqov Yosef 88c, in which the Ba'al Shem Tov is said to have called the daily *'Amidah* ''the true embrace and coupling'' is a paraphrase of such earlier sources as Zohar 2:128b, but with an important difference. To the earlier mystics, the coupling was envisioned as taking place *within* God; in the Hasidic reading, it is God and the worshiper who are locked in the embrace of intimacy.

81 Zawa'at RIVaSH 18a.

82 Keter Shem Tov 33a. The term *devequt* is central to Hasidic thought, particularly in the school of Dov Baer of Miedzyrzec, and is given many definitions in Hasidic literature. For a discussion of this term and its implications, cf. G. Scholem's essay ''Devekuth or Communion with God'' in *The Messianic Idea in Judaism*, pp. 203ff.

83 Or Ha-Emet 2b. The quotation is from the literature of Merkavah mysticism.

84 Liqqutim Yeqarim 15d.

85 Zawa'at RIVaSH 13a; Keter Shem Tov 39b-40a. The forces of evil are commonly described in Kabbalistic

sources as *qelipot* ("shells") which seek to hide the light of divinity from the world.

86 Zawa'at RIVaSH 4b. The quotation is from Psalm 35:10.

87 Ketonet Passim 43b. The right hand of God is traditionally associated with divine love, while the left signifies divine might and rigor.

90 Sefat Emet (by Meshulam Feibush of Brezhan), wa-era. Quoted in Sefer Ba'al Shem Tov, Noaḥ #105.

91 Divrey Mosheh 35b. The parable, attributed by the Ba'al Shem Tov to his brother-in-law R. Gershon Kitover, seems to recommend rapid prayer, so that distractions will not have a chance to enter the worshiper's mind. A shorter version of the same parable is used to prove a rather different point in Toledot Ya'aqov Yosef 194c.

93 Liqqutim Yeqarim 15c.

94 Liqqutim Yeqarim 3a; Or Torah 160b. The passage is a comment on Hillel's dictum in Avot 1:14, offering a strikingly radical re-reading of the original passage.

95 Ben Porat Yosef 88d. A comment on Exodus 34:3.

96 Liqqutim Yeqarim 15a; Keter Shem Tov 37b; Or Ha-Emet 83b.

97 Toledot Ya'aqov Yosef 67d. The quotation is from Mishnah Berakhot 4:4, here interpreted to mean that one should make the fixed prayer sufficiently flexible to allow for the special qualities of each day.

100 Liqqutim Yeqarim 3b. Truth, according to the rabbis, is God's royal seal.

101 Zawa'at RIVaSH 3b. The Cracow and other later editions read *bet ha-kenesset* ("synagogue") instead of *bet*

127

ha-kise' ("bathroom"), obviously a printer's error based on a confusion of abbreviations!

102 Liqqutim Yeqarim 2a.

103 Or Ha-Me'ir 1:10a. On early Hasidic attitudes toward esoteric prayer, cf. J. Weiss' article "The Kavvanoth of Prayer in Early Hasidism" in *Journal of Jewish Studies* 9 (1958). This text is discussed on pp. 179ff.

104 Zawa'at RIVaSH 14b; Liqqutim Yeqarim 17d. This text too is discussed in the article mentioned in the preceding note, p. 178.

105 Buzina Di-Nehora 54.

106 Zawa'at RIVaSH 7b.

107 Dibrat Shelomo 2:50b-51a. The reference is to the three prayers of the daily liturgy. The image of man as the King's gardener is well-known in Midrashic literature, based on an understanding of Genesis 2:15.

108 Kitvey Qodesh 9b.

109 Divrey Shemu'el 124. Another version of this parable is quoted by S. Y. Agnon in his *Atem Re'item*, p. 70.

112 Liqqutim Yeqarim 15b; Keter Shem Tov 37b-38a.

113 Degel Mahaneh Ephraim 131b. The passage reflects a deep and frightening awareness of the closeness between devotional states and other aspects of man's emotional life.

114 Keter Shem Tov 37b; Liqqutim Yeqarim 15b; Zawa'at RIVaSH 7b. Here the sources reflect two seemingly contradictory counsels. Could the latter be a warning against the dangers of the former?

115 Zawa'at RIVaSH 17b.

118 Or Ha-Me'ir 5:42b-c. The parable is quoted in the name of the Ba'al Shem Tov. The author of the Or Ha-Me'ir offers the suggestion that man must be blind to this world in order to see the other—an explanation which seems to escape rather than confront the frightening reality of this parable.

EDITIONS OF HASIDIC
WORKS QUOTED

'Avodat Yisra'el	Jerusalem, 1955
Ben Porat Yosef	Piotrkow, 1883
Buẓina Di-Nehora	Lvov, 1884
Darkhey Ẓedeq	Warsaw, 1877
Degel Maḥaneh Ephraim	Jerusalem, 1963
Dibrat Shelomo	Jerusalem, 1955
Divrey Mosheh	Israel, 196-? (Zolkiew)
Divrey Shemu'el	Jerusalem, 195-?
Hekhal Berakhah	Lvov, 1864
Ḥesed le-Avraham	Jerusalem, 1954
Hit'orerut Ha-Tefillah	Piotrkow, 1911
Keter Shem Tov	Beney Beraq, 1957
Ketonet Passim	New York, 1950
Kitvey Qodesh	Lvov, 1862
Liqqutim Yeqarim	Lvov, 1863
Maggid Devaraw Le-Ya'aqov	Jerusalem, 1954
Or Ha-Emet	Brooklyn, 1960
Or Ha-Ḥokhmah	Jerusalem, 1970
Or Ha-Me'ir	Israel, 1968 (Warsaw)
Or Torah	Jerusalem, 1968
Oraḥ Le-Ḥayyim	Jerusalem, 1960
Pitgamin Qaddishin	Warsaw, 1886
Sefer Ba'al Shem Tov	Szinervaraljan, 1943-Landsberg, 1948
Shemu'ah Tovah	Warsaw, 1938
Tif'eret 'Uzi'el	Tel Aviv, 1962
Toledot Ya'aqov Yosef	Jerusalem, 1966 (Korzec)
Toledot Yiẓḥaq	Warsaw, 1868
Torey Zahav	Mogilev, 1816
Ẓawa'at RIVaSH	Cracow, 1896

About the Authors

ARTHUR GREEN is Lown Professor of Jewish Thought at Brandeis University. He studied at Brandeis University and the Jewish Theological Seminary. He is a student of Jewish theology and mysticism who has sought to combine scholarly career and personal commitment. In addition to *Your Word Is Fire*, his works include *Seek My Face, Speak My Name: A Contemporary Jewish Theology* (Jason Aronson, 1992) and *Tormented Master: The Life and Spiritual Quest of Rabbi Nahman of Bratslav* (Jewish Lights, 1992). Dr. Green has served as president of The Reconstructionist Rabbinical College in Philadelphia and as associate professor of Religious Studies at the University of Pennsylvania, and has lectured widely in academic and communal settings.

BARRY HOLTZ is co-director of the Melton Research Center at the Jewish Theological Seminary of America and Associate Professor in the Seminary's Department of Jewish Education. He is the author of *Finding Our Way: Jewish Texts and the Lives We Lead Today* (Schocken Books, 1990) and the editor of *Back to the Sources: Reading the Classic Jewish Texts* (Simon and Schuster, 1984) and, most recently, *The Schocken Guide to Jewish Books* (1992).

Both of the editors were founding members of the Havurat Shalom community in Somerville, Mass., and contributors to *The Jewish Catalog*.

About JEWISH LIGHTS Publishing

People of all faiths and backgrounds yearn for books that attract, engage, educate and spiritually inspire.

Our principle goal is to stimulate thought and help all people learn about who the Jewish People are, where they come from, and what the future can be made to hold. While people of our diverse Jewish heritage are the primary audience, our books speak to the Christian world as well and will broaden their understanding of Judaism and the roots of their own faith.

We bring to you authors who are at the forefront of spiritual thought and experience. While each has something different to say, they all say it in a voice that you can hear.

Our books are designed to welcome you and then to engage, stimulate and inspire. We judge our success not only by whether or not our books are beautiful and commercially successful, but by whether or not they make a difference in your life.

We at Jewish Lights take great care to produce beautiful books that present meaningful spiritual content in a form that reflects the art of making high quality books. Therefore, we want to acknowledge those who contributed to the production of this book.

ART DIRECTION AND PRODUCTION
Rachel Kahn

COVER PRINTING
New England Book Components, Hingham, MA

PRINTING AND BINDING
Book Press, Brattleboro, VT

Add Greater Understanding to Your Life

JEWISH LIGHTS Classic Reprints

TORMENTED MASTER
The Life and Spiritual Quest of Rabbi Nahman of Bratslav
by *Arthur Green*

Explores the personality and religious quest of Nahman of Bratslav (1772–1810), one of Hasidism's major figures. It unlocks the great themes of spiritual searching that make him a figure of universal religious importance.
"A model of clarity and percipience....Utterly relevant to our time."
                                                            —*New York Times Book Review*
                6"x 9", 408 pp. Quality Paperback, ISBN 1-879045-11-7 **$17.95**

THE LAST TRIAL
On the Legends and Lore of the Command to Abraham
to Offer Isaac as a Sacrifice
by *Shalom Spiegel*

New Introduction by *Judah Goldin, Emeritus Professor, University of Pennsylvania*

A classic. An eminent Jewish scholar examines the total body of texts, legends, and traditions referring to the Binding of Isaac and weaves them all together into a definitive study of the *Akedah* as one of the central events in all of human history.
"A model in the history of biblical interpretation, and a centerpiece for Jewish-Christian discussion."—*Dr. Michael Fishbane, Nathan Cummings Professor of Jewish Studies, University of Chicago*

                6"x 9", 208 pp. Quality Paperback, ISBN 1-879045-29-X **$17.95**

ASPECTS OF RABBINIC THEOLOGY
by *Solomon Schechter*

Including the original Preface from the 1909 edition
& *Louis Finkelstein's* Introduction to the 1961 edition
with an important new Introduction by *Dr. Neil Gillman, Chair, Department of Jewish Philosophy, The Jewish Theological Seminary of America*
Learned yet highly accessible classic statement of the ideas that form the religious consciousness of the Jewish people at large, by one of the great minds of Jewish scholarship of our century.
"This is the only book on the theology of Judaism written 100 years ago that anyone can read today with profit." — *Jacob Neusner, Distinguished Research Professor of Religious Studies, University of South Florida*

"A better antidote could not be found for the still too prevalent Christian ignorance of the richness and depth of the Jewish heritage." — *The Rev. Dr. Paul M. van Buren, Honorarprofessor Of Systematic Theology, Heidelberg University.*

                6' x 9", 440 pp. Quality Paperback, ISBN 1-879045-24-9 **$18.95**

YOUR WORD IS FIRE
The Hasidic Masters on Contemplative Prayer
Edited and translated by *Arthur Green* and *Barry W. Holtz*

YOUR WORD IS FIRE
The Hasidic Masters on Contemplative Prayer
Edited & Translated with a New Introduction by Arthur Green & Barry W. Holtz

The power of prayer for spiritual renewal and personal transformation is at the core of all religious traditions. From the teachings of the Hasidic Masters the editors have gleaned "hints as to the various rungs of inner prayer and how they are attained." These parables and aphorisms of the Hasidic masters pierce to the heart of the modern reader's search for God.

                6"x 9", 160 pp. Quality Paperback, ISBN 1-879045-25-7 **$14.95**

Add Greater Understanding to Your Life

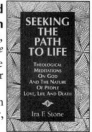

Spiritual Inspiration for Family Life

GOD'S PAINTBRUSH
by *Sandy Eisenberg Sasso*
Full color illustrations by *Annette Compton*

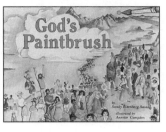

Multicultural, non-sectarian, non-denominational. Invites children of all faiths and backgrounds to encounter God openly in their own lives. Wonderfully interactive, provides questions adult and child can explore together at the end of each episode.
"The most exciting religious children's book I have seen in years."
—*Sylvia Avner, Children's Librarian, 92nd St. "Y," NYC*
"An excellent way to honor the imaginative breadth and depth of the spiritual life of the young."
—*Dr. Robert Coles, Harvard University*

For children K– 4 elementary.
11"x 8¹/₂", 32 pp. Hardcover, Full color illustrations, ISBN 1-879045-22-2 **$15.95**

THE *NEW* JEWISH BABY BOOK
Names, Ceremonies, Customs — A Guide for Today's Families
by *Anita Diamant*
A complete guide to the customs and rituals for welcoming a new child to the world and into the Jewish Community, and for commemorating this joyous event in family life–whatever your family constellation. Updated, revised and expanded edition of the highly acclaimed *The Jewish Baby Book*. Includes new ceremonies for girls, celebrations in interfaith families. Also contains a unique directory of names that reflects the rich diversity of the Jewish experience.

6"x 9", 272 pp. Quality Paperback, ISBN 1-879045-28-1 $15.95
Available October 1993

PUTTING GOD ON THE GUEST LIST
AWARD WINNER
How to Reclaim the Spiritual Meaning of Your Child's Bar or Bat Mitzvah
by *Rabbi Jeffrey K. Salkin*
Foreword by *Rabbi Sandy Eisenberg Sasso*
Introduction by *Rabbi William H. Lebeau, Vice Chancellor, JTS*

Joining explanation, instruction and inspiration, helps parent and child truly *be there* when the moment of Sinai is recreated in their lives. Asks and answers such fundamental questions as how did Bar and Bat Mitzvah originate? What is the lasting significance of the event? How to make the event more spiritually meaningful?

"Shows the way to restore spirituality and depth to every young Jew's most important rite of passage." — *Rabbi Joseph Telushkin, author of* Jewish Literacy
"As a Catholic clergyman who has helped prepare young people for confirmation, I find Rabbi Salkin's book to be a source of inspiration and direction." — *Msgr. Thomas Hartman, co-host, "The God Squad"*

6"x 9", 184 pp. Hardcover, ISBN 1-879045-20-6 **$21.95**

6"x 9", 184 pp. Quality Paperback, ISBN 1-879045-10-9 **$14.95**

SO THAT YOUR VALUES LIVE ON
Ethical Wills & How To Prepare Them
Edited by *Rabbi Jack Riemer & Professor Nathaniel Stampfer*

A cherished Jewish tradition, ethical wills, parents writing to children or grandparents to grandchildren, sum up what people have learned and express what they want most for, and from, their loved ones. Includes an intensive guide, **"How to Write Your Own Ethical Will,"** and a topical index. A marvelous treasury of wills: Herzl, Sholom Aleichem, Israelis, Holocaust victims, contemporary American Jews.

6"x 9", 272 pp. Hardcover, ISBN 1-879045-07-9 **$23.95**

6"x 9", 272 pp. Quality Paperback, ISBN 1-879045-34-6 **$16.95**

Motivation & Inspiration for Recovery

RENEWED EACH DAY
Daily Twelve Step Recovery Meditations
Based on the Bible
by *Rabbi Kerry M. Olitzky & Aaron Z.*

VOLUME I: Genesis & Exodus
Introduction by *Rabbi Michael A. Signer*
Afterword by JACS Foundation

VOLUME II: Leviticus, Numbers & Deuteronomy
Introduction by *Sharon M. Strassfeld*
Afterword by *Rabbi Harold M. Schulweis*

Using a seven day/weekly guide format, a recovering person and a spiritual leader who is reaching out to addicted people reflect on the traditional weekly Bible reading. They bring strong spiritual support for daily living and recovery from addictions of all kinds: alcohol, drugs, eating, gambling and sex. A profound sense of the religious spirit soars through their words and brings all people in Twelve Step recovery programs home to a rich and spiritually enlightening tradition.

"Meets a vital need; it offers a chance for people turning from alcoholism and addiction to renew their spirits and draw upon the Jewish tradition to guide and enrich their lives."
—*Rabbi Irving (Yitz) Greenberg, President, CLAL,*
The National Jewish Center for Learning and Leadership

"Will benefit anyone familiar with a 'religion of the Book.' Jews, Christians, Muslims. . . ."
—*Ernest Kurtz, author of* Not-God: A History of Alcoholics
Anonymous *&* The Spirituality of Imperfection

"An enduring impact upon the faith community as it seeks to blend the wisdom of the ages represented in the tradition with the twelve steps to recovery and wholeness."
—*Robert H. Albers, Ph.D., Editor,* Journal of Ministry in Addiction & Recovery

Beautiful Two-Volume Set.
6"x 9", V. I, 224 pp. / V. II, 280 pp., Quality Paperback, ISBN 1-879045-21-4   **$27.90**

ONE HUNDRED BLESSINGS EVERY DAY

Daily Twelve Step Recovery Affirmations Reflecting Seasons of the Jewish Year

by *Dr. Kerry M. Olitzky*
with selected meditations prepared by *Rabbi James Stone Goodman,*
Danny Siegel, and *Rabbi Gordon Tucker*
Foreword by *Rabbi Neil Gillman,*
The Jewish Theological Seminary of America
Afterword by *Dr. Jay Holder, Director, Exodus Treatment Center*

Recovery is a conscious choice from moment to moment, day in and day out. In this helpful and healing book of daily recovery meditations, Kerry Olitzky gives us words to live by day after day, throughout the annual cycle of holiday observances and special Sabbaths of the Jewish calendar.

For those facing the struggles of daily living, *One Hundred Blessings Every Day* brings solace and hope to anyone who is open to healing and to the recovery-oriented teachings that can be gleaned from the Bible and Jewish tradition.

4¹/2" x 6¹/2", Quality Paperback, 416 pp. ISBN 1-879045-30-3
$14.95

Motivation & Inspiration for Recovery

TWELVE JEWISH STEPS TO RECOVERY
A Personal Guide To Turning From Alcoholism & Other Addictions...Drugs, Food, Gambling, Sex

by *Rabbi Kerry M. Olitzky & Stuart A. Copans, M.D.*
Preface by Abraham J. Twerski, M.D.
Introduction by Rabbi Sheldon Zimmerman
Illustrations by Maty Grünberg
"Getting Help" by JACS Foundation

A Jewish perspective on the Twelve Steps of addiction recovery programs with consolation, inspiration and motivation for recovery. It draws from traditional sources, and quotes from what recovering Jewish people say about their experiences with addictions of all kinds. Inspiring illustrations of the twelve gates of the Old City of Jerusalem.

Experts Praise *Twelve Jewish Steps To Recovery*

"Recommended reading for people of all denominations." — Rabbi Abraham J. Twerski, M.D.

"I read Twelve Jewish Steps with the eyes of a Christian and came away renewed in my heart. I felt like I had visited my Jewish roots. These authors have deep knowledge of recovery as viewed by Alcoholics Anonymous." — Rock J. Stack, M.A., L.L.D. Manager of Clinical/Pastoral Education, Hazelden Foundation

"This book is the first aimed directly at helping the addicted person and family. Everyone affected or interested should read it." — Sheila B. Blume, M.D., C.A.C., Medical Director, Alcoholism, Chemical Dependency and Compulsive Gambling Programs, South Oaks Hospital, Amityville, NY

Readers Praise *Twelve Jewish Steps To Recovery*

"A God-send. Literally. A book from the higher power." — New York, NY
"Looking forward to using it in my practice." —Michigan City, IN
"Made me feel as though 12 Steps were for me, too." — Long Beach, CA
"Excellent–changed my life." — Elkhart Lake, WI

6" x 9", 136 pp. Quality Paperback, ISBN 1-879045-09-5 **$12.95**

RECOVERY FROM *Codependence*
A Jewish Twelve Steps Guide to Healing Your Soul

by *Rabbi Kerry M. Olitzky*
Foreword by *Marc Galanter, M.D., Director,*
Division of Alcoholism & Drug Abuse, NYU Medical Center
Afterword by *Harriet Rossetto, Director, Gateways Beit T'shuvah*

For the estimated 90% of America struggling with the addiction of a family member or loved one, or involved in a dysfunctional family or relationship. A follow-up to the ground-breaking *Twelve Jewish Steps to Recovery*.

"The disease of chemical dependency is also a family illness. Rabbi Olitzky offers spiritual hope and support." —*Jerry Spicer, President, Hazelden*

"Another major step forward in finding the sources and resources of healing, both physical and spiritual, in our tradition." —*Rabbi Sheldon Zimmerman, Temple Emanu-El, Dallas, TX*

6" x 9", 160 pp. Hardcover, ISBN 1-879045-27-3 **$21.95**
6" x 9", 160 pp. Quality Paperback, ISBN 1-879045-32-X **$13.95**

The Kushner Series

GOD WAS IN THIS PLACE & I, i DID NOT KNOW
Finding Self, Spirituality & Ultimate Meaning
by *Lawrence Kushner*

Who am I? Who is God? Kushner creates inspiring interpretations of Jacob's dream in Genesis, opening a window into Jewish spirituality for people of all faiths and backgrounds.

In a fascinating blend of scholarship, imagination, psychology and history, seven Jewish spiritual masters ask and answer fundamental questions of human experience.

"A brilliant fabric of classic rabbinic interpretations, Hasidic insights and literary criticism which warms us and sustains us."

—Dr. Norman J. Cohen, Dean, Hebrew Union College, NY

"Rich and intriguing." —M. Scott Peck, M.D., author of *The Road Less Traveled*

6"x 9", 192 pp. Hardcover, ISBN 1-879045-05-2 **$21.95**

6"x 9", 192 pp. Quality Paperback, ISBN 1-879045-33-8 **$16.95**

HONEY FROM THE ROCK
An Introduction to Jewish Mysticism
by *Lawrence Kushner*

An introduction to the ten gates of Jewish mysticism and how it applies to daily life.

"Quite simply the easiest introduction to Jewish mysticism you can read."

"*Honey from the Rock* captures the flavor and spark of Jewish mysticism. . . . Read it and be rewarded." —Elie Wiesel

"A work of love, lyrical beauty, and prophetic insight. "—Father Malcolm Boyd, *The Christian Century*

6"x 9", 168 pp. Quality Paperback, ISBN 1-879045-02-8 **$14.95**

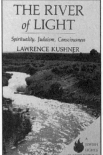

THE RIVER OF LIGHT
Spirituality, Judaism, Consciousness
by *Lawrence Kushner*

A "manual" for all spiritual travelers who would attempt a spiritual journey in our times. Taking us step by step, Kushner allows us to discover the meaning of our own quest: "to allow the river of light—the deepest currents of consciousness—to rise to the surface and animate our lives."

"Philosophy and mystical fantasy...exhilarating speculative flights launched from the Bible....Anybody—Jewish, Christian, or otherwise...will find this book an intriguing experience."—*The Kirkus Reviews*

"A very important book."—Rabbi Adin Steinsaltz

6"x 9", 180 pp. Quality Paperback, ISBN 1-879045-03-6 **$14.95**

Spiritual Inspiration for Daily Living

THE BOOK OF WORDS
Talking Spiritual Life, Living Spiritual Talk
by *Lawrence Kushner*

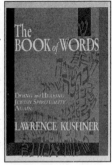

In the incomparable manner of his extraordinary *The Book of Letters: A Mystical Hebrew Alphabet*, Kushner now lifts up and shakes the dust off primary religious words we use to describe the spiritual dimension of life. The *Words* take on renewed spiritual significance, adding power and focus to the lives we live every day.

For each word Kushner offers us a startling, moving and insightful explication, and pointed readings from classical Jewish sources that further illuminate the concept. He concludes with a short exercise that helps unite the spirit of the word with our actions in the world.

6"x 9", 176 pp. Hardcover, two-color text ISBN 1-879045-35-4 **$21.95**

Available September 1993

Sample pages from *The Book of Words*

THE BOOK OF LETTERS
A Mystical Hebrew Alphabet
by *Rabbi Lawrence Kushner*

In calligraphy by the author. Folktales about and exploration of the mystical meanings of the Hebrew Alphabet. Open the old prayerbook-like pages of *The Book of Letters* and you will enter a special world of sacred tradition and religious feeling. More than just symbols, all twenty-two letters of the Hebrew alphabet overflow with meanings and personalities of their own.

Rabbi Kushner draws from ancient Judaic sources, weaving Talmudic commentary, Hasidic folktales, and Kabbalistic mysteries around the letters.

"A book which is in love with Jewish letters." — Isaac Bashevis Singer

• Popular Hardcover Edition
6"x 9", 80 pp. Hardcover, two colors, inspiring new Foreword.
ISBN 1-879045-00-1 **$24.95**

• Deluxe Gift Edition
9"x 12", 80 pp. Hardcover, four-color text, ornamentation, in a beautiful slipcase.
ISBN 1-879045-01-X **$79.95**

• Collector's Limited Edition
9"x 12", 80 pp. Hardcover, gold embossed pages, hand assembled slipcase. With silkscreened print.

Limited to 500 signed and numbered copies.

ISBN 1-879045-04-4 **$349.00**

To see a sample page at no obligation, call us

Order Information

# Copies		$ Amount

• *The Kushner Series* •

# Copies		$ Amount
_____	The Book Of Letters	
_____	• Popular Hardcover Edition, $24.95*	_____
_____	• Deluxe Presentation Edition w/ slipcase, $79.95, *plus* $5.95 s/h	_____
_____	• Collector's Limited Edition, $349.00, *plus* $12.95 s/h	_____
_____	The Book of Words, (hc) $21.95*	_____
_____	God Was In This Place And I, i Did Not Know, (hc) $21.95; (pb) $16.95*	_____
_____	Honey From The Rock, (pb) $14.95*	_____
_____	The River Of Light, (pb) $14.95*	_____
_____	The Kushner Series - All 5 Books - *marked with an asterisk above*- $93.75	_____

• *Other Inspiring Books* •

# Copies		$ Amount
_____	Aspects Of Rabbinic Theology, (pb) $18.95	_____
_____	God's Paintbrush, (hc) $15.95	_____
_____	The Last Trial, (pb) $17.95	_____
_____	Mourning & Mitzvah, (pb) $19.95	_____
_____	The *NEW* Jewish Baby Book (pb) $15.95 *Available October 1993*	_____
_____	Putting God On The Guest List, (hc) $21.95; (pb) $14.95	_____
_____	Seeking The Path To Life, (hc) $19.95	_____
_____	So That Your Values Live On, (hc) $23.95; (pb) $16.95	_____
_____	Spirit Of Renewal, (hc) $22.95	_____
_____	Tormented Master, (pb) $17.95	_____
_____	Your Word Is Fire, (pb) $14.95	_____

• *Motivation & Inspiration for Recovery* •

# Copies		$ Amount
_____	One Hundred Blessings, (pb) $14.95 *Available October 1993*	_____
_____	Recovery From Codependence, (hc) $21.95; (pb) $13.95	_____
_____	Renewed Each Day, 2-Volume Set, (pb) $27.90	_____
_____	Twelve Jewish Steps To Recovery, (pb) $12.95	_____
_____	The Jerusalem Gates Portfolio (all 12 prints), $49.95 *50% SAVINGS*	_____
_____	The Jerusalem Gates Portfolio, Any 3 prints $25.00	_____

List numbers here: _____ _____ _____

For s/h, add $2.95 for the first book, $1 each additional book.

Total _____

Check enclosed for $_____ *payable to:* JEWISH LIGHTS Publishing.
Charge my credit card: ❏ MasterCard ❏ Visa ❏ Discover ❏ AMEX

Credit Card #_____Expires _____

Name on card _____

Signature _____ Phone ( ) _____

Name _____

Street _____

City / State / Zip _____

Phone or mail to: JEWISH LIGHTS Publishing
Box 237, Sunset Farm Offices, Route 4, Woodstock, Vermont 05091
Tel (802) 457-4000   *Fax* (802) 457-4004
Toll free credit card orders (800) 962-4544 (9AM–5PM EST Monday–Friday)
Generous discounts on quantity orders. SATISFACTION GUARANTEED. Prices subject to change.
AVAILABLE FROM BETTER BOOKSTORES. TRY YOUR BOOKSTORE FIRST.